THE PERFECT PROMPT

A collection of poems to inspire your creativity

Jen Elvy

Copyright © 2020 Jen Elvy

All rights reserved

The characters and events portrayed in this book are fictitious. Any similarity to real persons, living or dead, is coincidental and not intended by the author.

No part of this book may be reproduced, or stored in a retrieval system, or transmitted in any form or by any means, electronic, mechanical, photocopying, recording, or otherwise, without express written permission of the publisher.

ISBN-13: 9798580122441
ISBN-10: 1477123456

Cover photo by Jen Elvy
Library of Congress Control Number: 2018675309
Printed in the United States of America

To all who create, this is for you.

CONTENTS

Title Page	
Copyright	
Dedication	
How to Use This Book	1
Wooden Winter Hut	2
Wooden Winter Hut - Next Steps	3
Through the Keyhole	4
Through the Keyhole - Next Steps	5
Gates	6
Gates - Next Steps	7
Happy Place	8
Happy Place - Next Steps	9
Enchanted House	10
Enchanted House - Next Steps	11
Behind the Door	12
Behind the Door - Next Steps	14
Enchanted Spells by the Lake	15
Enchanted Spells by the Lake - Next Steps	17
Pebbled Footsteps	18
Pebbled Footsteps - Next Steps	19
Stairway	20

Stairway - Next Steps	22
Woodland Arch	23
Woodland Arch - Next Steps	24
The Snow Queen	25
The Snow Queen - Next Steps	26
House in the Tree	27
House in the Tree - Next Steps	28
Acknowledgement	29
About The Author	31
Books By This Author	33

HOW TO USE THIS BOOK

Of course, you can enjoy the poems as they are if you wish and you needn't do more than that. In fact, I'd love you to do that. These poems were written to entertain and capture imagination, after all. However, they were also written as questions, with information deliberately left out in order to spark your creativity and encourage you to produce some work of your own, be it a piece of creative writing or a piece of artwork such as a painting, a sketch or even a collage. This is why, after each poem, I have added the following sections:

Points to Ponder

These are questions to ask yourself. These questions could be the starting point to you creating a piece of writing or art based around the poem.

Over to You

This section contains prompts for your creativity and ideas to try. You may have your own ideas so feel free to try them too. I'd love to see what you create.

I sincerely hope you enjoy this book as much as I enjoyed writing it and I hope you find some inspiration within these pages.

Jen

WOODEN WINTER HUT

I took a walk on a winter's night.
The snow was sparkling in the moonlight.
The air was crisp and the trees were still.
I trekked my way across the field until
I came to some trees and beyond them I saw
Something that I simply couldn't ignore;
A little wooden hut with fairy lights all round
And when I got closer, guess what I found?
Footprints leading to the small wooden door
And the lights casting shadows on the forest floor.
I started to ponder this magical sight
That stood before me on a winter's night.
Who lives in this hut? Are they inside?
Is it a resting place? Or where they reside?
A million questions entered my mind
And the answers I truly wanted to find.

WOODEN WINTER HUT - NEXT STEPS

Points To Ponder

What do you think happens next?

Does the narrator venture inside this hut?

If so, what do they find?

Over To You

Create a piece of artwork based on the scene that the narrator sees before them.

Create a piece of artwork based on what you think happens next in the story.

Write a poem further describing the hut that the narrator discovers.

What would the scene look like in another season? Describe using words or art.

Write a poem or a story describing what happens next.

THROUGH THE KEYHOLE

Through the keyhole, I can see
A pretty fairy waving at me.
She is tall; she has blonde hair,
With eyes a shade of blue so rare.

Through the keyhole, I can see
A bunny rabbit, as white as can be.
His eyes are tiny; his ears are long.
I want to sing him a happy song.

Through the keyhole, I can see
The greenest, tallest, old oak tree.
Its trunk is thick; it stands so proud.
I think it's trying to touch a cloud.

Through the keyhole, what will you see?
Will you see an animal running wild and free?
Will you see a fairy or perhaps a little elf?
Have a little look and see for yourself.

THROUGH THE KEYHOLE - NEXT STEPS

Points To Ponder

What would you see through the keyhole? Close your eyes and set your imagination free.

What does the door look like? Is it large and wooden? Is it metallic? Or is it a fairy door? What is the scene outside?

Over To You

Choose one of the verses and create a piece of artwork based on the scene that the narrator describes.

Create a piece of writing or artwork based on what you would see if you looked through the keyhole.

GATES

Standing there at the gates of dread,
A million thoughts fill each little head.
They think they're going to be turned into frogs
Or, worse than that, get eaten by dogs.

What will they find when they reach that threshold?
They know it won't be a pot of gold.
They're certain that there are bad things to come
And they all just want to go home to their mum.

But what if it's not as bad as they fear?
What if they are made welcome here?
What if they find a friendly queen;
The most beautiful lady they've ever seen?

Or what if they find a lonely bird,
Whose song is the sweetest they've ever heard?
Who knows, when they get to the house, what they'll find?
They'd better hurry before they change their minds.

GATES - NEXT STEPS

Points To Ponder

What would the children find at the house?

Would it be delightful? Or enchanting? Or would it be haunting and frightening?

Sometimes all is not as it first appears, but sometimes it is!

Over To You

So, through the gates they start to wander;
A determined stride, no time to ponder.

Continue the poem using the above lines. Or alternatively, think of your own opening lines. You could even write it as a story.

Create a piece of artwork showing the house that you think the children see before them.

Create a piece of artwork to show what you think would happen next.

HAPPY PLACE

Do you have a happy place
Where you like to go?
Somewhere you can seek out
In sun, rain or snow?

Do you have a happy place
Where you can hide out,
When life just gets too sticky
And you want to scream and shout?

Do you have a happy place?
Is it near or far?
Can you walk right to it,
Or do you need a car?

Or is your little happy place
Somewhere deep within,
Where you can reach your happy thoughts
And hear them dance and sing?

HAPPY PLACE - NEXT STEPS

Points To Ponder

What is your happy place?

Is it an actual place or is it imaginary?

Or could it be just a peaceful and calm place in your mind?

Over To You

My happy place is a bench by the lake
Where time out for myself I can take.
I sit peacefully and watch all the trees
Waving gently in the summer breeze.

Continue this poem or write your own about your happy place. It can rhyme but it doesn't have to.

Alternatively, create a piece of artwork showing your happy place.

ENCHANTED HOUSE

Who lives in the enchanted house?
Is it a little gnome with a pet mouse?
Or is it where fairies come home to bed,
To sleep off the magic and rest their heads?

Who lives in the house with the red, pointy roof?
Is it the elf, who seems quite aloof,
And hides away among many a tree?
Is that why nobody's ever been to tea?

Who lives in the house with ivy around the walls?
Is it where the goblins come when the evening falls?
Or where fairies gather to learn their magic spells?
I know that someone knows the truth but no one ever tells.

ENCHANTED HOUSE - NEXT STEPS

Points To Ponder

Can you picture this house in your mind?

What other enchanting features does it have on the outside?

Who lives inside this house?

What magical things happen there?

Over To You

Write a poem or story describing the outside of the house using the ideas in the poem along with your own.

Who lives inside the house? Write a poem or a story to tell us what happens inside the house.

Create a piece of artwork showing either the house in the poem or your own ideas for an enchanted house.

Imagine your own enchanted house and write a poem or story about it. What does it look like on the outside? Who lives inside? What happens in the house at night? What about during daylight?

BEHIND THE DOOR

They climbed the stone steps
To the big, brown door.
What was behind it?
They wanted to explore.

A tree with purple leaves
Was shedding for Fall.
What a strange tree!
It intrigued them all.

They knocked on the door;
There came no reply.
Was anyone in there?
They gave it one more try.

There was still no answer.
What should they do?
Try and open it, perhaps?
Would they walk straight through?

The door was stiff;
It stood solid and still.
To make it budge
Would take some skill.

But what was that noise?
The strange creaking sound?
Would someone let them in?
Could they look around?

Finally, the door opened
And a voice said "Come in!
We've been waiting for you.
Shall we begin?"

BEHIND THE DOOR - NEXT STEPS

Points To Ponder

Who is speaking in that final verse?

Why have they been waiting?

What do they want to "begin"?

And who are the characters attempting to open the door? Are they children? Adults? Teens?

Over To You

Who are the characters in the poem? Draw them or write about them, perhaps creating character profiles.

Who answers the door and speaks to the group? Create a piece of artwork or write about the person. Is there anyone else inside with them? If so, you could include them too.

What happens next? Write a story, write a poem, or tell the story through art.

ENCHANTED SPELLS BY THE LAKE

Beyond the rippled waters of the lake
There is a tranquil and enchanted place,
Where magical spells are cast against
Every member of the fairy race.

Who would cause such mischief?
Who would even care
What the little fairies do
In their magic lair?

Is it the witches, who are fed up
Of fairies thwarting their plans,
And have decided to take matters
Into their own hands?

Could it be the wizards
With their cloaks of gold,
Their long, grey beards,
Their actions so bold?

Or is it the goblins,
All shifty and cruel,
Their darting green eyes

JEN ELVY

Eyeing every jewel?

Who would do such a thing
To the gentle fairy clan?
Who in the world would hatch
Such a cunning plan?

Co-written by **Dan Elvy**

ENCHANTED SPELLS BY THE LAKE - NEXT STEPS

Points To Ponder:
Who is casting the spells against the fairies?

Is it someone suggested in the poem?

Or someone who the narrator doesn't suspect?

What sort of magical spells were cast against the fairies?

Over To You:
Tell the story of the group of people who cast the spells against the fairies. Tell it from their point of view. Use rhyming verse if you wish. Let the reader know the reasons behind the spells and describe the spells and the effect they have on the fairies.

Create a piece of artwork based on this poem. You may choose to focus on groups mentioned in the poem, e.g. wizards or goblins.

Write about, or create a piece of artwork based on, what spell you would cast against the fairy race.

PEBBLED FOOTSTEPS

Where do the pebbled footsteps go?
To a secret island in the snow?
Where it's always winter and never spring?
Where unicorns walk and ice fairies sing?

Where do the pebbled footsteps lead?
To where the worker fairies can do a good deed?
Where each deed is rewarded with a spell
And an enchanted, golden, spiral seashell?

Do you think they lead to a wooden hut,
Where elves make sweets of coconut?
Do you think they lead to a statue of stone?
Or could they lead to a dinosaur bone?

There's just one way to solve this mystery;
Follow the footsteps and see what you see.
There really is no reason to be afraid.
Go on, hurry, or the magic will fade!

PEBBLED FOOTSTEPS - NEXT STEPS

Points To Ponder

Where do the footsteps lead?

Do they lead to somewhere suggested in the poem?

Do they lead somewhere else in your imagination?

Over To You

Create a piece of artwork showing the pebbled footsteps.

Write a story or poem about where the footsteps lead.

Create a piece of artwork to show where the footsteps lead.

STAIRWAY

As I climbed the mossy staircase,
I saw a speck of light,
Which bathed the gloomy cave
With a radiance so bright.

I wondered what it was
That shone so bright and bold.
Was it a doorway
To a room with lots of gold?

The light grew bigger as I approached,
The stairs so deep and winding.
My feet were getting tired
But the light was so spellbinding.

I couldn't wait to get to the top
To see what lay ahead.
A dragon breathing fire?
A giant in his bed?

Finally, I was there at the top,
The light blinding my way.
As I dared to step forward,
I saw a golden sleigh.

A voice spoke in whispers;
"Follow me," it said.
Then I saw a man
(but he wasn't wearing red).

He said, "Come to my kingdom,
I have everything you need.
Step onto my sleigh,
Led by my trusty steed."

I did as he requested
And we went on our way;
One man and a white horse
And a shimmering sleigh.

STAIRWAY - NEXT STEPS

Points To Ponder

Who is the man in the story?

Where does he take the narrator?

Who is the narrator? A child? An adult?

How did they end up in the cave?

Over To You

Create a piece of artwork showing the scene in the poem.

Create a piece of artwork showing what you think happens next.

Write a poem or story based on what happens next.

Write about the narrator of the poem. Create a character profile. Tell their back story.

WOODLAND ARCH

Have you seen the arch in the wood?
It is where a gentle wizard once stood.
He would welcome the magic folk.
The breeze would blow his bright blue cloak.

Beyond the arch was a party for all;
Folk from around the land would call.
There'd be tasty things to eat
And lots of magic as a treat.

But one day, alas, some dreadful happenings
Put an end to years of cosy gatherings.
Never again, beyond the arch, would they meet.
Never again would they taste food so sweet.

WOODLAND ARCH - NEXT STEPS

Points To Ponder

What happened to put an end to the gatherings?

Was it a person that caused it or was it a chain of events?

Over To You

Create a piece of artwork showing one of the wizard's historical gatherings, or alternatively, simply showing the wizard himself.

Why did the gatherings end? Tell the story, write a poem or create a piece of artwork.

THE SNOW QUEEN

Climb the steps,
Go through the arch.
Go early in the year,
No later than March.

Be sure to tread softly
Through the snow.
Stay very quiet
And mind how you go.

Stick to the path;
Don't stray too far.
At night time, search
For a sparkly star.

Follow the path
In the snow so clean,
And eventually
You'll reach the Snow Queen.

THE SNOW QUEEN - NEXT STEPS

Points To Ponder
What does the Snow Queen look like?
Why should you go no later than March?

What would the Snow Queen say to you?

What are her surroundings like?

Over To You
Create a piece of artwork showing part of the journey to the Snow Queen.

Create a map showing the whole journey.

Create a piece of artwork showing what happens when you reach the Snow Queen.

Write a story about a visit to the Snow Queen. Write it as a poem if you wish. Describe the Snow Queen and her surroundings.

HOUSE IN THE TREE

Do you know who lives
In the house in the tree?
Do you think they are
Just like you and me?

Do they like to travel
And build unique homes?
Do they like to collect
Quaint garden gnomes?

Have they a dog,
Or a cat or a mouse?
What strange creatures
Dwell in that house?

Do you like the decorations?
And do you agree
That they look like those that hang
From a Christmas tree?

Such a joy to see
Such a unique abode
In a dense forest
Far from the road.

HOUSE IN THE TREE - NEXT STEPS

Points To Ponder
Where is this house?
What does it look like?

Who lives there?

What happens inside?

Over To You
Create a piece of art work of the House in the Tree.

Write a poem about who lives in the house. Create the characters.

Something peculiar happens inside the house. Tell the story; write a poem; create a piece of artwork. Would it be out of the ordinary to the characters in the story? Or just to you and me?

ACKNOWLEDGEMENT

There are many I would like to thank for the production of this book. Firstly, thank you to my Instagram writing community. You are all so dear to me. You have inspired and supported me so much over the past year or so and you always have fantastic things to say about my work and, for that, I am so very thankful.

A special mention to Tessy Braun, who has given me lots of advice about my work and about self publishing and also helped me think of the title of this book. You were the first to read out my work on an Instagram Live, you have put me in touch with the most wonderful community and have always encouraged and inspired me. Thank you so much.

Another special mention goes to my team at Myth and Lore. Thank you so much Sarah, Morden, Kaila and Lainy. Your prompts have always inspired me and you are all so supportive of my work. And I was honoured to join the team as a curator earlier this year.

Over the past year, I have posted the odd prompt on social media and I want to say thank you to those who have responded. It was so rewarding to read or see your responses and it has really encouraged me to get this book written and out there.

Thank you also to all friends and family who have supported my work, both in person and on social media. Your support means everything.

Thank you so much to my wonderful husband, Dan for his creative input, his love and his support for my work. I love you with all my heart. Thank you to my boys as well for being my energy and my muse. Mummy loves you lots.

Finally, thank you to those who have taken the time to order and read this book. I hope you have enjoyed it and I hope that the prompts have inspired you.

ABOUT THE AUTHOR

Jen Elvy
Jen works in education and lives in Kent with her husband and two boys. She loves using and creating prompts for artists and writers, which was her inspiration for this book.

BOOKS BY THIS AUTHOR

A Fantasy Feast
A collection of fantasy poetry. escape from the here and now with a feast of enchanted poetry. Perfect for bedtime reading.

A Hunt For Sparkled Treasures
A ten part narrative poem about a hunt for jewels.

Printed in Great Britain
by Amazon

19794808R00031